FRAGRANT AUNT NELLIE

AND 99 OTHER SHORT POEMS TO READ IN THE LOO

A LIGHT-HEARTED LOOK AT MODERN LIFE

BY

JESSICA JONES

DEDICATION

This book is dedicated to my late father, Dr David Oldroyd.

CONTENTS

CHAPTER 4. CONCEPTS, CATS AND MISCELLANY

CHAPTER 5. BEING BRITISH AND THE TWO R'S 93

ACKNOWLEDGMENTS

Thanks to my husband Alan, and family and friends for their encouragement and tolerance, as it became apparent that there were going to be a lot of poems.

Thanks too to Gold Wind Ltd. for taking on 'Aunt Nellie,' who hopes to be back for more.

Thanks also to the late Monica McLaughlan for her generous bequest, which has been used to fund publishing expenses.

CHAPTER 1

LOOK THIS WAY

1. THE INSTAGRAM EYEBROW

The Instagram eyebrow's a curious thing.
There aren't any spaces; they're all coloured in.
Back in the eighties all eyebrows were thin,
from plucking and tweezing the brows (and the chin).

Plucking and tweezing and waxing yourself:
you must, to avoid ending up on the shelf.
Also the men aren't allowed to be lax,
in attending to backs and to sacks and to cracks.

But now for us oldies no more need to worry.
At our time of life it's OK to be hairy
Both upstairs and down, let our gardens be full.
There's no Instagram madness, and our lives are not
dull.

2. TATTOOS

And now to tattoos
my attention has wandered.
The inking of bodies:
'But why?' I have pondered.
The urge for a body
all covered in doodles
of dragons and boobies
and swear words and poodles,
will always elude me.
Especially when aged
this art gets all fuzzy
and saggy and faded.

Some chaps on the knuckles
will have 'hate' and 'love' writ;
and hippy types covered
in symbols and Sanskrit;
a spider's webbed visage
worn proud like a scar;
obligatory dolphin
peeks over the bra.
As already mentioned,
in those who are inky,
in no time at all
these pics will be wrinkly.

3. SELFIES

I never take selfies;
no pouting for me.
My arms are too short
and my height's five foot three.

These pics are unkind
when you're past twenty-five.
Our wrinkles and chins
from being alive

for so many years
are much magnified.
But we like to pretend
that we're ageing with pride.

Beware electronic
devices and see
the iPad and Kindle
and phone on your knee,

when not yet ignited,
the smooth surface glowing,
is just like a mirror,
your own selfie showing.

The first time I saw this
was rather a shock;
my non-youthful features
were cruelly mocked.

With those whom you love
there's no need to dissemble;
they don't give a stuff
about what you resemble.

4. NEVER BEEN AIRBRUSHED

I've never been airbrushed; fake tan's not my friend.
I'm not a celeb, nor wish to pretend

that I have a hope of attracting a glance,
like those on the top shelf, not in their pants.

I've seen what the light in the ceiling uncovers.
I'll stay in my clothes and leave it to others

to get out their bits of which they're most proud.
I'll stay under wraps and remain in the crowd

of people who don't like displaying their wares
and attracting attention and horrified stares.

5. NIP AND TUCK

Should I have a nip and tuck?
I've reached that age when liposuc-
tion seems an option for celebs,
(more important than us plebs)
when they reach this time of life,
compelled to undergo the knife,
or Botox, boob implants and fillers.
Some of these we know could kill us.
When they're lying on the beach
shiny faces, bum a peach,
necks betray that they are lying,
nipples gravity-defying.
Rounded silicone enhanced bits
don't fall sideways to the armpits.

6. HIPSTERS AND YOUTHS

It seems that hipsters with huge beards
look to some a little weird.
But they say it's just a fashion
that they grow a massive 'tache on
upper lips. Now thus adorned
by some partners now are scorned;
they prefer their faces bare
without this Captain Birdseye hair.

What about the footwear some choose?
Long and shiny, pointy elf shoes,
sticking out 'neath skinny jeans
that fit so tight. Have they not seen
quite what they look like in a mirror?
Surely it's a fashion error,
or is it me who's out of date?
Flares will come back – just you wait.

Think this is bad? There's so much more.
A dressing faux pas to deplore:
the low-slung trouser's just not right,
with yards of underpant in sight,
and worn by youths to show they're hard.
But this impression is not shared.
To normal folk who've thought this through,
perhaps you have a low IQ.

7. GOOD FOR YOUR AGE

'Good for your age.'
When you're at that stage,
this comment's meant
with kindest intent

to make you feel good,
but worry you should:
there's hidden content
in this compliment.

The speaker well knows
what time has bestowed –
a wrinkled visage
and décolletage.

But hold up those chins.
Stride out on those pins,
with zimmer or cane.
Ignore all the pain,

and live for today;
there's no other way.
It's time to have fun;
your work is now done.

8. PUMPING IRON

Pumping iron in the gym
is a way to keep you slim.
There's no need for steroid use,
magic pills or fancy juice.
Demonstrate that you're no slouch;
no need for a posing pouch,
baby oil or bottled tan
just to show that you're a man,
whose body is a temple now,
biceps, abs and lats endowed.
Take care not to go too far;
your pals preferred you as you were.
The pumped-up look just makes them worry,
you'll now shun their pint and curry.

9. AGEING SKIN

If you get past forty, your skin will start to sag,
gravity will say hello and all things downwards drag.
Your frowns will turn to wrinkles, and seborrhoeic
warts
arrive and look like dried on lumps, and cover these
you ought.
But celebrate the ageing bod; enjoy it all in private;
varicosities are fun when hosiery's connived at.

Bright red dots you'll note one day, suddenly
emerging:
Campbell de Morgan spots – named by a famous
surgeon.
Harmless, but they can alarm when noticed in the bath.
Take them to the surgery to give your doc a laugh.
Actinic keratosis, quite common in the bald,
is a bit more worrying, but please don't be appalled.

Although it's a pre-cancer, there's treatment to apply,
onto the bonce, do more than once, and leave until
it's dry.
The ageing skin is itchy; it's proper name: pruritis.
It's best if you can keep it moist and ward off
dermatitis.
Drink water and apply sufficient cream emollient.
Use this lots to maintain a robust integument.

10. FOLLICLE MATTERS

Women have great choices
of colour, length and curl;
granny bubbles, thigh-length locks
or pigtails for a girl.
But if your white hair's now dyed black,
please keep on top of it,
or else a badger you'll look like
and fashion crime commit.

Don't bother with a rug, chaps,
you could just wear a hat.
your looks won't be enhanced by
a densely woven mat.
It doesn't matter if you're bald,
just smile and you'll fulfil
all you need for happiness,
your follicles can chill.

11. ATTRACTION

In order to provoke desire,
one needs to possess or acquire
certain attributes; not lack
these vital aphrodisiacs:

elongated lower limbs,
eyelids that are darkly rimmed,
lashes much enhanced with gunk.
If you're a chap, best be a hunk,

with pecs of steel and abs if poss,
and girls remember your lip gloss.
GSOH will mitigate
when good looks don't predominate.

With hods of cash you might get by;
this never fails to catch the eye
of suitors seeing their solution;
it's because of evolution.

12. SHOPPING FOR CLOTHES

If you dislike shopping for frocks,
be happy in trainers and socks.
There's no need to try to squeeze
bits of you into these
pencil skirts, ball gowns and smocks.

When you need a new pair of shoes,
but can't afford posh Jimmy Choos,
or Louboutins either;
you've only a fiver,
best go to eBay; what's to lose?

Let's say you're a chap and need undies,
just shop any day – even Sundays,
and smuggle the budgie,
in boxers if pudgy.
Change these every day, like your mum says.

13. BAD FASHION

Sartorial standards will drop
if you buy velour stuff from a shop,
or shell suits all shiny
that soon become grimy.
Attempts to impress will then flop.

Animal print is no better.
With this you won't be a trend setter.
Ditto leather trews;
such things never choose.
From ankle chains best stay unfettered.

The baggy grey tracksuit is worn
by criminals (usually torn).
Step back from culottes;
this item is not
invented to flatter the form.

With leggings in Lycra on show,
a thing or two you need to know:
no sweaty bits please;
ensure no one sees
the worst fashion crime: camel toe.

CHAPTER 2

HEALTH AND HABITS

14. ODE TO PUDDINGS

Who'd love a spotty dick today,
with custard all around?
Who cares about the waistband toll;
what of an extra pound?

In these days of fitness fads
I yearn for Mother's puds.
Low fat this, no sugar that;
who wants theses tasteless duds?

So listen well to Hollywood,
and Leith and Mary Berry.
Celebrate your inner chef
and make your mealtimes merry.

15. SUGAR AND GLUTEN

'Sugar and gluten
are bad for our bods.'
So say the experts,
and everyone nods.
We must give up alcohol,
cakes and such foods.
What's left to eat
that has not been eschewed?

I'd quite like a dumpling,
a roll or a pie.
If no one is looking,
I'm going to defy,
the rules of the health Nazis,
they don't know best.
But now it's a struggle
to put on my vest.

And when it's near Christmas
all this just gets worse:
there's stollen and pudding –
we'll be fit to burst.
And then in the new year
the gyms will not fail
to get those of us in
who've stood on the scales.

16. INSOMNIA

When you lie awake at night, the counted sheep long gone,
your restlessness has reached its height and meditation's done,

it's time to choose a strategy of which there are a number:
a nightcap or a glass of milk might aid you in your slumber.

But it's for sure I know a time you'll never fail to snooze:
if you tune in to listen to a round of PMQs.

When you yawn the whole day through, and wish you were a cat,
with no responsibilities, 'cept lounging on a mat,

that cappuccino late last night you sadly now regret,
and vow to do decaf next time, so night-time needs are met.

But what of those who wander while sleeping like a log,
diverse misdemeanours undertaken in this fog?

If mischief might amuse you, pretend to do the same.
Have fun with what's forbidden. Somnambulance
then blame.

17. REIKI AND ASTROLOGY

Reiki and astrology –
truly bonkers stuff!
We see convincing evidence
that it's a load of guff.

Homeopathy attempts
to suck you in with tales
that water holds a memory,
but in this aim it fails.

And as for iridology,
and crystals sagely dangled,
the science is not sound,
of these modalities newfangled.

Rubbing with essential oils
might soothe an anxious mind.
Phrenology to locate bumps
used to seem refined.

For all your cash the outcomes
are effective, as we know,
but no more than a jelly bean,
and just a placebo.

18. DRUGS

If reality's not where you want to be
Then journey using pharmacology.
Get off your face on Charlie or on skunk,
or by other means escape the funk.
These days a smorgasbord is there for you.
The benzos, opiates and even glue
can transport you to realms you'd never see
without these substances, like spice and E.
A purchase from a dodgy chap will do.
Or see your doc and fake a pain or two.

19. CIGARETTES

Fresh air's overrated;
I'd rather smoke a tab.
With all their tar and nicotine,
they're really rather fab.

You wouldn't understand;
you folk who say it's bad.
We have to die of something
and my habit makes me glad

to wake up every morning
and light a little stick
of joy, and breathe in deeply.
They never make me sick;

except that first encounter
at school with all rest;
the peer pressure mounting
to do what they thought best.

To fund this little pleasure
has cost me hods of cash.
But if I had my time again
I'd do it in a flash.

I'm shunned by kith and kin;
to some I'm a pariah.
But I'm prepared to choose the phlegm
and light my little fire.

20. MEN'S BITS

Testicular atrophy trips off the tongue,
but is not a desirable state.
It refers to the shrinkage of bits down below,
and makes it a problem to mate.

So stay off the steroids and booze in excess,
and let your anatomy thrive.
For good procreation and fun recreation
keep spermatozoa alive.

It's best not to smoke or to have heart disease,
and try to avoid, if you can,
obesity and diabetes; keep healthy
the blood vessels in your old man.

21. EATING UNHEALTHILY

If you want a muffin top,
gorge on noodles and don't stop.
Pasta, garlic bread and beer
help some rolls of flesh appear.
Cheesecake with ice cream is fun;
makes your buttons come undone.
For an extra special bulge,
in huge pies you should indulge.
Lots of sugar in your drinks
Has with weight gain causal links.
Visits to the doc increase
for those who're classified obese.
Diabetes, not desired,
when your pancreas gets tired,
can afflict those large of girth.
NHS advice is worth
your attention, and I hope it's
lowering risks of mitosis.
Experts say we're what we eat.
If that's true and we're complete-
-ly made of food then I'm quite pleased
that what I'm made of must be cheese.

22. HYGIENE

It shouldn't be too hard to keep your nooks and crannies clean.
In loos you'll find a basin for hand washing when you've been.

Most people access shower, bath and soap quite easily.
Yet even well-off folk assault us olfactorily.

And then there are the types whose clothes are worn for weeks on end.
They have a special odour that from far away offends.

When underneath a nail a blackened crescent can be seen,
you try hard not to contemplate where those hands might have been;

'specially if they're serving food and you have hunger pangs.
But now you've changed your mind and say we'll have the bill now thanks.

And as for those who try to mask the stench with perfumed spray;
be under no illusion, this is not at all ok.

Beneath a layer of discount scent are cloying pheromones,
as unwashed folk are not disguising minging undertones.

23. LOOK AFTER YOUR BODY

Look after your body; it looks after you.
Don't fill it excessively; think when you chew.
When it's not meal time step back from the fridge,
or you'll get too heavy by more than a smidge.

Be careful when glugging the hop and the grape;
if sober you'll still enjoy laughter and japes.
A tipple is fine and can add to the fun,
but have a few days when your intake is none.

Stop fretting 'bout cellulite, wrinkles and droop.
best not to lose fat eating just cabbage soup.
Enhancing your features with slap is OK,
but cosmetic surgery's not a good way

to alter your looks, as you can't change your mind;
your startled new look is now frozen in time,
your face stiff and shiny, but neck has gone slack.
Your massive boob implants have slipped round the
back.

And what's with this unhealthy photoshop meme,
changing your shape so you're not what you seem.
It might not be surgery but you can't conceal
from people who know you, your picture's not real.

The body's amazing and is so much more
than just what it looks like. I'd like to implore
the peer-pressured young folk to wander outdoors,
and take fewer selfies; go forth and explore

the world and it's wonders and feel more alive.
Be kind to your body and mentally thrive.
In Latin 'twas said by one wise with insight:
'mens sana in corpore sano' – quite right!

24. PLEASE DON'T GO TO A&E

Please don't go to A and E
unless your need is urgent.
Do go with strokes and heart attacks
or swallowing detergent.

It isn't there for colds and cuts
and piles and nappy rash.
If you turn up with something mild
they'll spot this in a flash.

They'll put you in a cubicle
and take off all your clothes.
And make you wear a paper dress
through which your bottom shows.

25. DOCTOR'S RECEPTIONIST

Be nice to the doctor's receptionist, please!
She's trying to help you get healthcare with ease.
You might not believe it
when she makes you sit
for hours among those with flatus disease.

A doctor's receptionist does work she loves,
to keep punters happy, but she's not above,
getting one up on you
if you make the air blue.
She'll make sure the doc knows it's time for the
gloves.

26. DOCTORS' WRITING

Doctors' writing is a mystery.
It goes back quite far in history.
It's a skill in med school learned.
Codes in Latin, kudos earned.
Lay folk might be mystified;
how're their drugs identified.
Chemists too must learn this skill.
How to pluck the chosen pill
from apothecary shelves,
having understood, themselves,
potions, tinctures, sig ut dict,
mitte sixty, as it's writ.
Now though they have come undone:
computer scripts spoil all the fun.

27. BE A GOOD PATIENT

Be a good patient; be nice to the doc.
Please have a bath if removing a sock,
or showing an armpit or rash in the folds
of skin on your belly. Be kind to the nose
of the medical person in that room for hours.
Don't leave them great clouds of body unshowered.
Remember your time slot and please plan ahead.
It's not realistic to hope that the med-
-ic has all of the answers for all your life's ills.
For years of bad habits there's no magic pill.
Some folk are unlucky in life's lottery.
But if you stay away from things that are le-
-thal, like alcohol, baccy and drugs from the street;
avoid stress, wear seatbelts and watch what you eat,
no sugar, no additives, bacon or spam,
you might be around for your telegram.

28. CONTRACEPTION

Contraception is a must
if you feel you're not yet fussed
on changing nappies, wiping bums.
Put off being dad or mum.
Many methods you could take:
pills or implants, or just make
a cup of cocoa by yourself.
Condoms waiting on the shelf;
till moment intimate arrives.
You don't want a big surprise:
blue line on a chemist's stick.
In the morning there'll be sick.
You have both advice not heeded;
replication has succeeded.

29. HOSPITAL VISITING

Hospital visiting can be quite fun,
if you adopt an approach that to some
might seem disrespectful, but it's no false claim:
a good sense of humour is what keeps you sane.

You mustn't arrive before you're allowed
near the bedside, and don't form a crowd.
Two at a time and leave all pets at home.
No smuggling Fido in or he might roam

and leave an unwelcome moist offering.
Come on your own but remember to bring,
not grapes or some blooms or a sweet sticky bun,
but carry some items to leave when you're done:

a fake pile of poo to place at the scene,
a cushion that parps or a rude magazine.
There's always a story nearby to eavesdrop;
some bodily function that's started to stop,

and drama unleash on the family next door.
You know that tomorrow you'll come back for more.
It's better than telly and now you can say
your family duty is done for the day.

30. SLEEP

Too much or too little with nowt in between;
when folk talk of sleep there's no comfortable mean.
It's been a bad night, or they've slept like a log,
or been kept awake by a neighbouring dog.

Now most folk drink caffeine, the nation's divided;
some say their espresso will keep them wide ey-ed
right into the wee hours; but others are smug
and claim they can sleep all night after a mug

of this dastardly brew. I can't see the appeal;
it's glugged by old Frenchmen with every meal.
You've seen what they look like when gathered round
boule:
as if they've not slept well since they were at school.

Some are convinced by a wee drink or two.
but sleep then's not proper; sadly it's true.
All those with small bladders must suffer the plight
of needing to visit the loo in the night.

One day of our bodies we'll all lose control;
need nocturnal trips to the porcelain bowl.
It's best to avoid any recall of dreams,
the content is always distressing and seems

real at the time, even though it's absurd,
the stuff conjured up's best unseen and unheard.
Necessity means that time spent in this way
for us to be healthy's a third of the day.

31. TEA

Earl grey, lapsang, camomile;
not for me, they just taste vile.
If a cup of builders' tea
is offered, then I'll sup with glee.
There's nowt so good to cheer the soul;
a steaming cup makes one feel whole.
Don't waste time with tiny glugs;
this joyful brew deserves large mugs,
not nano cups and spouts that spill
all over, so your cup won't fill.
How sad it seems tea bags have plastic
in their make up; time for drastic
action. Back to leaves we'll go.
The flavour's better, as we know.

32. PHOBIAS

Some of the longest and funniest words
relate to the things of which we are scared.

The 'phobia' suffix is added with ease;
Thus: genuphobia means fear of knees.

Acro – of heights and haemo – of blood;
alektorophobia's as clear as mud.

This means fear of chickens, we'd need to explain.
Next, ombrophobia means fear of rain.

Many of these are not easy to guess;
hypochondria is fear of illness.

This is the only one I've found so far
not ending in phobia. Fear of a car

is amaxophobia – comes from the Greek.
As all of these do. In public to speak

with fear is called Glosso – as you might have guessed.
But iatrophobia's the one I like best.

33. THE NHS

We're grateful for the NHS and all that it provides,
the hospitals and staff they have, and all the stuff
outside;

as most care happens not in here but in care primary,
and in your home, if there you're stuck, by team
community.

Don't let's go American and lose what we have now.
The vested interest politic ensures a mighty row.

And those with power and cash might win and their
own beds might feather;
we'll then fund our own cancer drugs and other stuff
forever.

The Yanks have some insurance schemes to cover
patients' backs;
But don't be fooled by this; so many still slip through
the cracks.

You might complain of waiting lists and cannot get a
slot,
when you decide to see the doc with nappy rash or
snot.

Don't head that way with minor rash, or cough or if
coryzal;
this just exacerbates for folk the waiting list reprisal.

And don't be cross with 111; they do their best to
send
you to someone appropriate when you're at your wit's
end.

We are lucky; we don't have to walk for many hours,
or sell our souls, to get healthcare. The NHS is ours.

34. GLASSES

Short-sighted, long-sighted, astigmatism;
eyesight dysfunction like presbyopism:
all are amenable to some correction
with lenses and prisms for clever refraction.

Remember the spectacles with thick black rims,
when lenses like bottle ends made one look dim?
Technology's progress has improved the fate
of unlucky folk who could not get a date.

Aesthetics dictate you should not need to make
repairs with Elastoplast – that's a mistake.
And please don't be drawn to the habit invidious
of flip-up sunshades – they're simply quite hideous.

CHAPTER 3

LOOS AND LEISURE

35. MARRIED TO A MAMIL

I'm married to a M.A.M.I.L.
who's married to his bike.
Endurance like a camel,
on his velo not his trike.
This Middle-Aged Man in Lycra
disappears for ages,
and scales the heights of Mont Ventoux
and other grand tour stages.

His padded bum and helmet
are the outfit for this game.
He burns the miles and climbs the hills
in a circle till he's hame.
The refuelling process then takes place;
hide the cheese and toast!
But first, depleted fluids means
some beers are needed most.

36. MUSIC

Music music everywhere
and no place left to think,
It's in the shops, the gym, the bar,
pushing me to the brink.

My tolerance of youthful noise
is very low at best.
And now there's always video;
with no one in a vest!

The talented, those not so much,
are out there in their masses,
filling the airwaves with the sounds
that almost shatter glasses.

I'm a fogey, yes, I know,
but this was ever thus.
I'll buy some ear plugs when I go
next time out on a bus.

37. PUBLIC TOILETS

When e'er you visit a public loo,
spare a thought before you're through,
for all those people far afield
who have no paper roll to wield.
And as for those who live in France,
they have to do the hover dance.
I'm told Japan has got this sorted;
all their seats are automated.
Older folk remember Izal –
shiny paper! Yes, your eyes'll
not deceive you; it was true –
your grannie used this in the loo.
Only one sheet was permitted.
Thriftiness meant none was frittered.
We are lucky when we pee
now to go in luxury.

38. DRIVING

Now what about driving?
We all have our thoughts
on who does it well,
and who shouldn't have bought,
a massive Mercedes,
to show off with pride,
that they couldn't park
in a field, if they tried.

Some don't prefer
to sit in the back.
As these folk can drive
as if on a track.
As good as the Clarksons,
the Hammonds and Mays,
their reflexes honed
on the lanes on Sundays.

I know that my skills
are not up to this level.
I hesitate terribly,
foot on the pedal –
not on the right side;
the one 'neath my shoes
is the one on the left,
while my passengers snooze.

39. I'M NOT A STRICTLY FAN

I'm not a Strictly fan,
and don't get all the fuss.
I'm not the only one;
there are a lot of us.

We only move around
for function, not for fun.
We cannot bear the sounds;
when Strictly starts, we're done.

You'll find us in the pubs,
the cinemas and parks.
We tolerate the snubs
and Strictly fan remarks.

When we have fun we're still;
no wiggling of hips.
When we have time to kill,
a beer may pass our lips.

The fake tan and the glitter
the dazzle and romance,
makes us non-fans titter,
and we never want to dance.

It's Revel Horwood heaven,
Darcy shows her score,
then Bruno shouts: 'It's seven!'
And we rush for the door.

40. OPERA

Classical music is soothing to hear
But opera isn't my bag.
The screeching and wailing are harsh on the ear.
If I had my way, I would gag

the singers producing this racket.
They're able to make sounds no human detects.
The high pitch attained by this level of training
is audible only to pets.

The costumes are striking and on stage fantastic;
they move and expand with each song.
The dressmaker clearly needs lots of elastic
To make these constructions so strong.

Supporting the habitus common in singers
is not taken lightly you know.
Mechanical sturdiness must be constructed
when dressing the star of the show.

41. FANCY RESTAURANTS

It's not a joy to dine in style
if you are conscious all the while
of poncy waiters proffering
some quite egregious offering,

to try in vain to tempt the buds
of taste, when really all the puds
are made of foam and air and ice,
when what you want is something nice,

like spotty dick or apple tart
or frangipan to warm the heart.
The fancy sweets may not enlarge
the waistline but you will be charged

a fortune by the Michelin-starred;
no more credit on your card.
And guess what irritates me most?
When you get home you'll need some toast.

42. PORNOGRAPHY

When ankles were risqué and ogled for thrills
a lady retained her mystique.
But now a full frontal's the least we demand,
not happy with just a bum cheek.

Moreover, it's now an anatomy lesson;
you'll see things without underwear
in high definition and hairless; it's fashion
to epilate every last hair.

A glimpse of a curve could be so tantalising
in bodice laced up to the neck.
But now the full boobie is out there unshackled
so people can view the top deck.

Do try not to lose what is special for two
while spectating some unlikely coitus,
as those on the screen have possibly been
the victims of people exploiters.

43. DAYTIME TELLY

Get yourself a hobby;
anything will do.
Don't do daytime telly;
it's no good for you.

Watching people cooking,
baking cakes and pies,
private acts confessing
for all the nation's eyes,

TV gardeners lugging pots,
decking everywhere,
picket fencing sunspots;
no expense is spared.

Many years could pass,
watching all these shows,
or moronic quizzes.
Get old before you know.

Avoid the fate of many,
who this advice ignored,
spent their days addicted
to screen time for the bored.

You'll get square eyes,
and also dysfunction socially.
Mr Kyle and quiz hosts
will seem like family.

Eyeing up your dishes
with bargain hunters' zeal,
you'll try to get your pills from
TV docs who are not real.

44. TOUR DE FRANCE

Three weeks of exhausting stuff;
hardcore cycling for those tough
sportsmen wearing Lycra. Thighs
bulging but with arms the size
of tiny twigs. They'll never prize
open packs of crisps. They're wise

and know quite well that when they've ridden,
snacks like this are all forbidden,
as are things in Jiffy bags.
For T.U.E.s the rules are lax.
Pan y agua? That's allowed;
riding clean, of which they're proud.

Gone the days of Lance's rule.
Bags of blood and EPO fool
no one now. But still legit:
massage, ice bath, keeping fit.
Wiggins, Thomas, Froome and Yates.
Well done you Brits, we think you're
great.

45. HAIRDRESSERS

Cut and style, perm or dye,
choose your look and don't be shy.
Brace yourself for them to say:
'Are you going on holiday?'
While you sit and watch the clock
clever potions curl your locks.
'Neath the foils for tints and tones
tune in to the nearby drones
of private tales from other clients.
Experience this social science;
hear of lives like telly soaps,
of misdemeanours, fights and gropes.
Surely this is where you'll find
TV writers and their kind,
hearing plots for them to use
in future shows that we peruse.
Take care not to overshare,
or you'll find your life on air.

46. SUPERMARKETS

There's Asda and Aldi and Lidl and Morrison's too.
A Tesco and Sainsbury's and Waitrose you might find
near you.

But Booths you won't know if you live anywhere but
the Lakes.
Like Waitrose it's posh and only sells artisan bakes.

When shopping its best to avoid all the colourful
aisles.
They're laden with sugar and additives, packaged with
smiles.

They're not food at all and are marketed more to the
eyes.
Remember your grandparents; eat just like them to be
wise.

Stick to the bits at the edge of the store and just buy
from dairy, green grocer and butcher and baker. Pass
by

those things aforementioned, and any soft drinks in a
can.
Just eat proper food that would be recognised by your
gran.

Stay healthy and slim and be happy. Try not to be
dumb
about nutritious food. You can choose what to put in
your tum.

47. SKIING

Why would you bother to buy all the clobber
to wear for one week of the year?
Your cupboards are filled with items that thrilled;
now redundant extreme winter gear.

Yet many insist and cannot resist
the lure of the mountains and slopes.
Zooming down in the mist, sometimes breaking their wrist,
if they haven't yet mastered the ropes.

We wait in long lines for lifts through the pines
while smokers inhale one last puff.
On cables in chairs we glide through the air,
rejoicing in all this white stuff.

And after the fun and hours in the sun
(if you're lucky) there's much still to do.
Après ski's here, time for mulled wine and beer;
there's pasta and goulash for you.

And if you're intact, you'll then make a pact
to do it all over again.
You'll agree to repeat it despite the sore feet,
and like childbirth forget all the pain.

48. CARS

Oh, to be able to join in the fun
when chaps discuss cars and how well they now run.
Or not, some might say, of an Alfa Romeo;
instead they'd be driving a new Ford Mondeo.
They don't like a Nissan; too boring, no thrills.
But gets you there safely; who needs all the frills?

The Subaru turbos or straight six of Porsches;
the Vtec of Honda, should make us all cautious.
The speeds now attained on our slip roads astound.
Perhaps they're the best place to wait for the sound
of magnificent engines unleashed by the bold;
 all cares about mpg now put on hold.

All of this happens en route to the shops.
(Best go unaccompanied or the fun stops.)
Petrol heads, know that we have your game sussed.
Detours and errands and trips when you just
pop out for a short while, you're up to your tricks
of four-wheeled excitement, it's time for your fix.

49. FOOTBALL

The offside rule is not that hard
to understand, and there's no card
in yellow from the ref to say:
you've gone too far while ball's in play.
But you can disobey the law
of physics and land on the floor;

without a push, you're on your face,
no tiny bump impedes your pace.
You made a movement underhand
to dive and on the grass to land.
Contusion small you might sustain
on knee or shoulder, but remain

intact and win the upper hand.
A penalty you'll have; that's grand.
And later when the other side,
who saw your action, then decide
to pay you back, without a care,
you now complain: 'they broke my hair!'

50. TV DETECTIVES

Wallander, Luther, Sherlock and Tosh;
great TV cops, like Hieronymus Bosch,
keep us enthralled with their crime-solving skills.
We can't get enough on-screen serial kills.

Back in the day when The Sweeney was tops
there'd be repercussions from vexing the cops.
Frost had us all on the edge of our seats.
Starsky and Hutch were fast on their feet.

Crocker and Tubbs tackled men's fashion crimes.
Taggart and Burnside were drawn to the grime.
The low life there made for plots gritty and pacey.
Remember the women too; Cagney and Lacey.

For stuff inexplicable, Mulder and Scully.
To appreciate Gillian Anderson fully,
she played Stella Gibson so well in The Fall,
the coolest female TV cop of them all.

Breaking Bad's Shrader had character flaws,
but love him we did, just as we did with Morse.
Remember too Ironside, Kojak, Columbo;
when leaving he'd talk pretend mumbo jumbo,

confusing his perp, and arrest getting nearer,
his tactic is not unlike Geordieland's Vera.
For glorious scenery, Magnum's Hawaii
and Five-O's McGarrett 'neath tropical sky

could seek out a criminal, testing their skills;
surviving each week to give us more thrills.
Now there's a whole genre called Scandi noir. Oh,
I nearly forgot to include Monsieur Poirot.

51. RUGBY

Normal folk would step aside
and just be glad that they've survived,
when muscle mountains head their way.
It's said this oddball game they play
is one for gentlemen, not those
folk less refined, and round ball choose.

Much time they give to lifting weights,
and crashing into padded mates.
Some macho words, like ruck and maul
and scrum are used. But where's the ball
in these set pieces? All I spy
is mud and sweat and lots of thigh.

The Southern Hemisphere play well;
and many smaller isles excel,
where mesomorphs predominate,
their shape is good for number eight.
When rest is due; they've had too much,
The ball is wellied into touch.

52. PERIOD DRAMAS

Historical dramas are loved by so many
but don't float my boat in the least.
Our favourite actors, all in it together,
from regular duties released.

They squeeze into bodices, breeches and bustles,
attaching false beards as required.
The dialogue's hammy and over-emotive
and extra posh diction's acquired.

Great care is then taken so items are hidden
that no one's had time to invent.
Heaven forbid that a mobile is spotted
or tone heard when text message sent.

There's only one story: some lovers are thwarted,
and several key folk are dispatched.
All feuds are then ended and love stories mended,
and wrist-cutting tunes are then matched.

The worst of them all must be Les Misérables;
why spend a whole evening so sad?
But give me a thriller or serial killer;
for this light diversion I'm glad.

53. HOBBIES

Cross stitch or trainspotting,
bridge or archery;
folk can't wait to tell you,
enthusiastically,
of many hours devoted
to hobbies quite diverse.
Some might seem mind-numbing,
others somewhat worse:

if you take up potholing
or jumping from a plane,
people will be asking
if you're completely sane.
You could stick to mainstream,
do Spanish class, play footy,
cook Delia at weekends,
make sculptures out of putty.

But if you have an interest
that might not seem benign,
except to those like-minded
you've only met online,
you'd best turn off your webcam,
please heed this and be warned,
we might find out your spare time's
spent perusing dodgy porn.

54. TAPAS

Tapas means you have to share
what others choose. And as they're fair,
most diners then are too polite
and waste the last delicious bite.

The spinach comes out far too soon,
so best dig in your tiny spoon.
Don't wait for seafood, it's delayed,
the other dishes won't be made

till you've consumed your weight in bread.
This type of meal is one I dread.
They charge an arm and leg per course
for tiny portions on a sauc-

er. Better have a pudding then,
or still be peckish later when,
you're back at home and near the fridge
and can't resist a tiny smidge,

of cheese on toast, you might as well,
have stayed at home and watched the tell-
y, next time maybe go elsewhere,
enjoy a hearty meal; don't share.

55. AIRPORTS

Hols are fine but getting there's a pain;
sometimes we just need a break from rain.
We tend to travel by default on planes.
If only we had user-friendly trains.

Frustratingly all airports retail lots
of posh designer tat; and all the spots
where you might sit are occupied with stuff
of which I'm sure we all have quite enough.

A giant Toblerone is not a must.
Don't buy an ornament to gather dust.
The local tipple will at home taste vile
But these in airport shops still fill the aisles.

Gold and tasteless bling by WAGs are worn
So no need to your body thus adorn.
Be glad if you don't live a life in which
you're valued only by the fact you're rich.

CHAPTER 4

CONCEPTS, CATS AND MISCELLANY

56. THE WORLD IS STILL HERE

The World is still here, despite all the fear,
of climate change war and pollution.
But how long we've got
depends quite a lot
on finding a timely solution.

Too much heat and disease,
and absence of bees,
could wipe us all out in a flash,
then act soon we must
or we'll become dust
and all of our hopes turned to ash.

So, as I've inferred,
heed Attenborough's words.
Let's avoid an apocalypse soon.
There's only one Earth;
we know what it's worth.
We can't make a home on the moon.

Our future survival
if we're still alive'll
be down to the will of the crowd.
Let's do it for babies
and toddlers and maybe
make all of our grandchildren proud.

57. RELIGION

Zoroastrianism's a monotheist faith;
also known as Mazdayasna, so the wise ones saith.
Much more of a mouthful than the Hindus, Sikhs or
Jews.
Pick one that you can pronounce, you know from
which to choose.

You could become a Muslim, if you're prepared to do
without a bacon sarnie, and all alcohol eschew.
It might, however, happen that Buddhism floats your
boat.
But know that in the next life you might come back as
a goat.

Or you could be a Christian and turn the other cheek.
Sing hymns on a Sunday and glorify the meek.
You could though turn to weirder sects if these ones
make you bitter.
Or just invent another, then sit back and have a titter.

58. FLOWERS

Please don't give me flowers;
they're pretty, yes, I see.
But now I have to watch them die
and that's no fun for me.

I know you want to comfort;
I know that you're a mate,
but maybe bring some chocolate
instead, that would be great.

Especially don't bring lilies;
the smell just makes me cry.
They also drop that powder stuff
on clothes when you pass by.

If blooms arrive from someone
who's kind but not aware
that flowers, to me, should stay outside
and live long in fresh air,

I'll say my thanks and find a vase
and put them on display,
but rather you'd just bring yourself
next time you come my way.

59. CATS

If you're not a feline lover,
skip past this one, read another,
or you'll know that we're all nuts
about our cats, despite the guts
and other gory items brought
and laid as gifts that they have caught.

They lie on laps and beds and chairs,
on keyboards and the edge of stairs,
all innocent, their gorgeous faces
peek out from surprising places.
Often in a box they sit;
try in tiny sinks to fit,

hide 'neath beds when thunder claps.
They love to sprawl on books and maps,
especially those now in use.
Soft furnishings they will abuse.
They're free to come and go all day
and, happily, most choose to stay.

60. EASTER ETC.

Easter starts in January; you've just packed up the tinsel.
The eggs in shops and bunny ears this soon will make you wince. I'll
bet you post a Facebook pic bemoaning this is so.
And all your pals will 'like' and 'share', and apt emojis show.

There's then a lull of many months till Santa reappears.
Summer hols are spent away from retail onslaught fears.
But look! That yonder orange ball, indeed a lovely pumpkin.
It's one of many in our shops, and not put there for munching.

It's time for pets to stay indoors, the best place to survive,
as pyrotechnics light our skies before November five.
Then back to school, the zombie fest's already in full swing.
Beware the gruesome purchases that kids to school must bring.

For bats and witches, spiders' webs you don't have far

to look.

And ghouls and ghosts and blood and goths are seen in every nook.

You'd best arrange to be away, perhaps go out to eat, or sit in silent darkness while avoiding trick or treat.

And gradually Norwegian trees accumulate in piles.

Rich foods and booze emerge with stealth in supermarket aisles.

Your gifts are wrapped by Halloween, while Santa's still sedate.

Before you blink, back on the shelves is ovoid chocolate.

61. ARTISTS

Colours and shapes, unique representations,
set artists apart from their friends' occupations.
In two D or three, they bring joy to all places,
both inside and outside in wide open spaces.
A gift must be part of the brain they possess,
'cos when I do art it's all just a mess.

And most folk can't create stuff we want to see.
The daubings of lay folk are bad, usually.
But don't be a part of the emperor's new clothes,
and speak in superlatives when you see those
artworks you think that a child could have done,
with eyes shut and paint brushes slopped on for fun.

It's all a conspiracy; money is made,
when those call it abstract, who've skills in this trade.
Best stick to the pieces that bring you great pleasure.
They may cost a pound but they're ones that you'll
treasure.
And if you have loved ones with creative fervour,
support these fab people and nurture their oeuvre.

62. ASTRONOMY

Ponder astronomy,
when Mr Ptolemy
knew all the star stuff so far.
But in modern science,
we have the two Brians,
that's Cox and May, who know by far

the most 'bout the firmament.
From them we learn what went
on when Big Bang marked the onset.
That's if time exists;
indeed, some doubt persists –
time might indeed be a false concept.

If that seems confusing,
prepare for a bruising,
now all of your brain cells are in use:
some theorists claim
that dark matter's to blame,
and cosmic expansion continues.

63. SMELLS

Old spice, wet dog.
Cut grass, eggnog.
Bad breath, perfume.
Fag ends, smoke plume.
Peanuts, road tar.
Lipstick, new car.
Worn sock, cat's pee.
Burnt wood, mint tea.
Thai food, baked bread.
Fresh paint, babe's head.
Raw meat, thick stew.
Hair spray, shampoo.
Carpet, squeezed lime.
Bleached loo, fresh thyme.
Rose bush, Merlot.
Soft talc, cocoa.
Onion, stale ale.
Clean sheets, oxtail.
Earl grey, fake tan.
Cordite, human.

64. GEEKS

Geeks are our heroes.
They know the world's round.
We'd be in the dark
if they hadn't found,
we live on a ball
that orbits the sun,
and rotates as well
every day just for fun.

These masters of knowledge
in science immersed,
they understand numbers
and concepts diverse.
It's thanks to Prof Hawking
their voices are heard.
These type now are loved,
as they've always deserved.

65. DOGS

Fido the pooch comes in all shapes and sizes, from small
to quite large, but I'm sure that the dachshund's the cutest of all.
It's said they're a dog and a half long and half a dog tall.
When you're this adorable who cares 'bout catching a ball.

They're friends with retrievers and labradors, 'cept when they eat.
The latter have appetites with which most dogs can't compete.
But any of these will delight all the humans they meet.
They're ever so handsome and patiently wait for a treat.

We're all a bit nervous when alsatians great us as guests.
If you meet a rottweiler, best wait till time for their rest.
But boisterous jack russels are harmless, their owners attest.
And great danes are soppy but they can reach up to your chest.

Some folk choose pedigree breeds that are just like
soft toys.
Wanting attention, these breeds tend to make lots of
noise,
but brighten the lives as companions for young girls
and boys.
I mean of course shar pei, shih tzu, bichon frise and
samoyeds.

66. AMUSING ANIMALS

The kangaroo and camel
can't help but make us smile.
The sloth, giraffe and hippo
are hilarious. Yet while

I'm sure it's for some function
they look the way they do,
their certain raison d'être
is amusing me and you.

And what about the sea life,
the flat fish and the whelk,
the dogfish and the mussel,
the underwater elk?

I made the last one up;
but there are squid and octopus.
And best of all, please don't forget
the duck-billed platypus.

67. COMPUTERS

Words that were unknown before,
by adults born in days of yore,
like bits and bytes and input state,
are there to discombobulate.
Prefix kilo, mega, giga
tell us if the number's bigger.
Tera, peta, zetta use
when your entity is huge.
Spyware, malware, trojan, spam,
learn for your IT exam.
You'll become a cyber geek;
help folk whose stuff needs a tweak.
Usually this is simply done:
just a switch turned off then on.

68. PROGRESS IN REVERSE

Wouldn't it be funny to have progress in reverse?
We'd talk about the things that are not here now –
quite perverse:
'There used to be a method to talk to folk afar.
We used some special cable, and also had radar.

Back in the day the World Wide Web had info in a
sec,
with button or a voice command; you'd not believe
the tech.
With satellites up in the sky to help us navigate,
in vehicles that moved quite fast, we'd never get there
late.

We had the means to fight disease; do complex
operations,
scans and tests at our behest for health investigations.
We don't now know anatomy or healthcare. That'll
teach us!
'Cos going backwards in this way, we even miss the
leeches.

It's possible that earlier, when life was more advanced
(!)
we'd been beyond the galaxy, by other worlds
entranced.

We may have also had the means ourselves to
teleport;
to get from A to B, and thus to travel just by thought.

But now that we have only books, and those we're
losing fast,
we haven't got the means to look so far into the past.
We'll soon be using word of mouth and symbols
carved on rock.
Brush up on your caveman skills; of what remains,
take stock.'

69. EPONYMOUS ANATOMY

You'll never sit down on a Eustachian tube,
nor travel the circle of Willis.
A Purkinje fibre's not found in your clothes,
but you might have a tendo Achilles.

Wernicke's area's not on a map;
nor Broca's, nor McBurney's point.
And as for the apple of Adam, no greengrocer
stocks this. And as for the joint

and foramen of Luschka you'll have these, but no
need
to worry, they function OK
without intervention, like Sphincters of Oddi,
rest easy, they're working all day.

Lieberkühn's crypts are not on a list
of must-see spots in foreign lands.
A last-minute trip can never be booked
to the small islets of Langerhans.

A Graafian follicle isn't your hair;
it's where reproduction can start.
And the bundle of Hiss refers not to a snake
but to fibres at work in your heart.

Eponymous bits of the body amuse
and give medical students some fun.
And in among those I have used, you'll have spotted
the eighth is the fictional one.

70. WATER

I'd like to mention H2O.
A vital substance, as we know,
It's of this that we're mostly made;
more than half, the experts said.
This and more we learned at school.
Let's praise this simple molecule.
To swim though, is not without risk,
there's more than water in the mix.
Even if no one has peed,
there's mucus, sweat and dirty feet,
and probably Elastoplast,
now floating as you breaststroke past.
I'm not alone in this aversion.
A bath is my preferred submersion.

71. FLAVOURS AND TEXTURES

Fresh bread, white bait,
suet pudding, chocolate.
Fruit cake, roast lamb,
peanut butter, rhubarb jam.
Treacle, thick cream,
scones and butter, coffee steam.
Rhubarb, mincemeat,
lemon drizzle, sherbet sweet.
Nutmeg, cheese bake,
glass of sherry, wedding cake.
Red wine, warm mead,
liquorice and aniseed.
Custard, fruit flan,
maple syrup, marzipan.
Black tea, beetroot,
coconut and passion fruit.
Bovril, marmite,
if down under, Vegemite.
Walnut, stoned date.
Did I mention chocolate?

72. WINDOWS

The window inventor deserves to be praised
by all of us living in homes that are glazed.
We'd be rather nippy if we still had holes
to let in the light but also the cold.

A further progression is glazing that's double,
letting us live in a virtual bubble.
The sound of the streets seems further away;
the screeching of hen parties now kept at bay.

For privacy use frosted glass or a blind.
Avoid the net curtain, as neighbours unkind,
who've nowt else to do, can ogle with glee
the comings and goings that they can half see.

I haven't yet mentioned the window as art;
in churches vast works their great stories impart.
Computers have windows that help the screens stack;
a feature integral, unless you've a Mac.

We also have windows inside of our ear;
fenestra ovalis helps us to hear
by transmitting sound across miniature bones,
we enjoy or endure a vast range of tones.

73. PETS

Dog or cat or guinea pig,
rabbit, goldfish, mouse.
These are pets you might have had
living in your house.
These are all adorable,
but some unwisely choose,
to keep a pet tarantula –
what chaos when it's loose!
Some folk have not seen Attenborough
or other wildlife shows.
They splash out on a small reptile
forgetting that it grows.
Some critters like to live outside,
and this is just as well;
Vietnamese potbellied pigs
might make your sofa smell.
The stick insect's an easy pet
and can for few months live. It
tells you when its life is done
as dead ones don't eat privet.
Remember fondly all the animals
who've shared your home.
And take care not to damage theirs
when in the wild you roam.

74. PERIODIC TABLE

Hydrogen, radium, lithium, tin,
is not the right order for elements in
the table that's laid out by structure in rows
and columns, or groups. As everyone knows,
the number of protons gives each one its place.
Discovering all of them's been a long race.
Over a hundred of these have been found.
There might be some others; keep looking around.
If you find a new one, unique, not the same,
as all of the rest, it'll get a fun name.
Thulium, hafnium names used so far,
and others, seaborgium, dubnium are,
hard names to recall. Organesson's fab;
this is the latest; t'was made in a lab.
Those with loose atoms are called allotropes;
different neutrons, these are isotopes,
And while on this topic, let's stop wasting helium,
needed, but rare on earth, just like promethium.
Plutonium's name's not from a cartoon,
but after the round body far from the moon,
No longer a planet, but fascinates all,
far out in the Kuiper belt, reasonably small.
Some gases are noble; they're stable and glow.
Ubiquitous neon's the star of the show.
It can get confusing as metals and gases
are in it together with differing masses.

75. BIRDS

There's no albatross in the garden,
no bald eagles munching our seeds,
no ptarmigan being suspicious
of cats lying low in the weeds.

These birds are all safe from attention
of predators, feline and small.
There's no camera clicking disturbing
their peace, as they're not here at all.

But through kitchen windows we're lucky;
of types of birds we can see lots.
As sparrows and blue tits aplenty
bring joy while we're rinsing the pots.

The blackbird and chaffinch and robin
are seen in our gardens a lot.
Hats off to the minuscule dunnock
whose libido attains the top spot.

Less popular magpies and seagulls
behave like the louts of the sky;
but their aerobatic manoeuvres
make us wish that we too could fly.

76. DOG POO

Some don't like the smell of curry; no spiced items in their food.
But nothing quite compares with what we notice when a dog has pooed.
If you're careless, step in error; squash a beige or pale brown mound,
't won't be long before the smell makes it quite clear what you have found.

We're grateful for a patch of grass; we scrape away with bits of wood.
But you will never lose the scent; you'll still detect in what you've stood.
A tiny blue bag looks appealing, when it's hanging from a tree.
On approach it's not a flower, leaf, or wee lamp that we see.

A bag or excrement was left, by someone with an odd idea:
'I think that I'll wrap up this poo and then I'll leave it hanging here.'
It may be these artistic souls are adding colour where they roam.
But please, if you are one of them, just pick it up and take it home.

CHAPTER 5

BEING BRITISH AND THE TWO R'S

77. UP AT THE END

When did we start to go up at the end?
Just like the Aussies, heaven forfend!
It's seemingly jolly but gets on my wick.
And adds to the onslaught of linguistic ticks.
I have not a gripe with our friends from the south,
but prefer not to hear this out of the mouths
of those in the media and now on the phone
when speaking with young people. Am I alone?
When will it end, this inflection? Not yet,
as: 'please could I have?' becomes 'please can I get?'
And 'woke' is a word whose usage is heightened.
We don't need this word; we have one: 'enlightened'.
The language must move on, I know, and we're liable,
or else we'd have words that are just in the Bible.

78. GOING FORWARD

'Going forward' used to mean
moving on from where you've been.
Now it's added in the gaps
when someone's short of words, perhaps.
It's a phrase that irritates,
and one that grammar Nazis hate.
Ubiquitous it is not yet,
unlike the use of 'like'. I'll bet
it won't be long before it's joined
by loathsome phrases not yet coined.

79. YOU'RE NOT A PROPER GEORDIE

You're not a proper Geordie
if you weren't born near the Tyne.
But you can learn the lingo
and get along just fine.

Ye'll larn the Geordie bible,
and quert it to yer mates,
and gan oot on the lash
with wor lass on a date.

If you're a monkey hanger,
you mustn't tell a soul,
as this is what they call
all folk from Hartlepool.

It's a tale from years ago:
a monkey came ashore.
They hanged him as a 'Frenchy' spy;
a crime, these day, for sure.

Let's not forget the Mackems,
who live astride the Wear.
These jolly folk will chat and joke;
their accent's very queer.

It seems they can't say 'toilet';
'torlet''s what you'll hear.
And when they talk of 'yesterday'
It's more like 'yesterdear'.

Now if you're from the 'Borough,
a Smoggie's what you're called.
The reason why eludes me,
and please don't be appalled,

as this nickname is really
a compliment, you see.
When you drive through this thriving town
you'll see their factories.

80. WERE YOU AROUND IN THE SEVENTIES?

Were you around in the seventies?
P'haps you recall
the colours of clothing and curtains
and carpets and all

were mustard and khaki and orange
and yellow and brown,
like the crushed velvet jacket
you lovingly wore into town.

We chose avocado for basin
and shower and loo.
Large patterns with swirls on
and furnishings garish of hue.

Hair piled up high, and eyeshadow
that had to be blue.
Miniskirts higher than stocking tops;
knickers on view.

No Instagram there to inform us
of what we should wear,
so photos stay hidden
of fashion crimes of yesteryear.

81. TODAY I'M FEELING ENGLISH

Today I'm feeling English.
Anyone for tea?
Let's listen to the Archers;
have scones and jam at three.

I love to see a big red bus,
a phone box, an ice cream van,
a London taxi just for us;
and don't forget the milkman.

Remember not to fly a flag
that's red and white. It's racist,
and folk will think you're bigoted
And say you're a disgrace. It's

best to love the simple things
like Yorkshire puds and stew.
Discuss the weather; when you shop,
be sure to form a queue.

82. THE DREADED CHRISTMAS LETTER

The dreaded Christmas letter
is upon us once again.
The round robin epistle
(never written with a pen).

All typed up, the details
of the past year, to impress,
of kids and jobs and pets and hols –
you'll only hear the best.

We'll never hear of granny's piles
or uncle's bankruptcy.
Auntie's misdemeanours
will be sworn to secrecy.

Tarquin won the Nobel Prize;
Jocaster's a brain surgeon;
Daddy conquered Everest;
babe's genius is emerging:

she learned to dance at seven months.
Speak Latin? Piece of cake.
She'll sit maths A level next month.
Don't fret, they're mostly fake.

They're just like all the rest of us,
but clever when they write
to all those folk they never see;
their real lives out of sight.

83. BRITS ABROAD

Brits abroad are splendid folk and much misunderstood.
We cannot talk in other tongues, but if we could we would.

Instead we speak up very loud when chatting to the locals,
and shout what are to native ears impenetrable vocals.

When we're abroad our lack of language skills can let us down.
If they hear us they'll think that Basil Fawlty is in town.

Have you heard most English folk when we attempt to utter, all
that we have learned to speak in French, we struggle with the guttural,

and softened Gallic R; we lack the oral apparatus.
And this is why we rarely try – we don't want them to hate us.

84. LITTER

Municipal flowers in neat little rows,
standing like soldiers, planted by those,
who work for the council and all dressed in green.
These elves of the parish,
you know when they've been.
The verges are dotted with brilliant hues,
to cheer the minds of passers who view

their glorious uniforms scattered all round.
You'd surely miss out were they not in the ground.
But ponder a mo' what else can be seen
on pavements we find that things aren't quite so
green,
but dappled with gum and fag ends and dregs
of leftover meals from McDonald's and Greggs.

How sad that no fine is enough to prevent
discarding of items with careless intent.
But fly tipping's worse and in most people's minds
these lazy and ignorant folk should be fined.
I hope one day on a solution we'll stumble,
but meanwhile I think we should call in a Womble.

85. FRAGRANT AUNT NELLIE

Fragrant Aunt Nellie
lives in the Mews.
Nivea moistened;
wears slippers, not shoes.

When you go to visit
you have to accept
bosomy greetings,
at which she's adept.

She'll slip you a tenner
for candy and treats.
But first you must sit
on her museum seats,

till your bottom is numb,
and hear all her tales
of when she was young.
And while she regales

you till you could yawn,
but stifle you must,
or she'll bring down uncle
now turned to dust,

who rests in a jar,
right next to her bed.
She'll share all the news
of when they were wed.

But never forget
the duty you owe
to that generation
who fortitude showed.

They're tough as old boots,
having lived long and thrived
in adverse conditions;
they more than survived.

86. HOLIDAYS

Whither will you travel
when freedom comes your way?
From daily burdens rest awhile
until another day.

Will you go to Europe
or stay in the UK?
Or will you venture further
from our continent to stay?

Why, though, will you travel,
when all you need is here?
Our telly and our countryside
and proper tea and beer.

The folk elsewhere will wonder,
puzzled frowns on all,
at our peculiarities
and fashions that appall.

The many pills and potions
needed for your trip;
the sunscreen, deet and ketchup
and flask of tea on hip,

are cumbersome to say the least,
but crucial to a Brit.
And as for socks and sandals,
our fashion choices, fit

for our shores only, really,
like Bognor, Poole and Bath.
So best to hol just down the road;
Stay here and have a laugh.

87. APOSTROPHES ETC.

An out of place apostrophe offends.
So too do other lazy language trends.
Some word shortening renders me irate,
but guess I understand 'deteriate'.
There are 'pecific' sins that make me wince.
No need for a 'sikth' sense when in an ins-
-tant you can spot the error spoken there.
Like folk who speak of 'tret' when they've had care;
The constant 'like' that's used in place of 'said'
And 'nuculer', of course, makes me see red.
'Particuly' is not a proper word.
And don't say 'think to' as that's just absurd.
And when you've sent a text, you must be clear
to say 'I texted', not 'I text', for fear
of causing folk who English love to hear
correctly used. Please don't offend the ear.

88. BREXIT

'Unexpected item in the bagging area.'
This and other phrases are not music to our ear.
'Your call is in a queue; we've not forgotten you.'
And now that 'leaves are on the line' we know we'll
be stuck here.

Maybe when we Brexit this will all be even worse.
The shopping queues and public loos will cause us all
to curse.
Or will we greet this blip with a stiffened upper lip,
And stand in line as chaos reigns, no euros in our
purse?

There might be no more croissants, and maybe no
baguettes,
no Perrier or Evian, just eau from the faucet.
And say adieu to owning a little country gîte,
as Albion Perfidious decided to Brexite.

89. ENGLISH PLACE NAMES

There's no place like England for names that are quaint
of places we live in. What pictures we paint
of Constable Burton and Stow on the Wold,
of thatched Nether Wallop, and also we're told

of Pucklechurch, Plumpton and Lickfold and Throop.
And well may you smile as there's also a Droop.
The first a location near Affpuddle boasts.
The latter's in Dorset, so nearer the coast.

Of Climping and Diddling you may not have heard.
Of Papplewick, Thrumpton and Wetwang, no word.
Their presence a joy to discover, and smile
about names of small places throughout this green isle.

90. WHAT ARE THESE 'BEETLES' DADDY?

'What are these 'beetles' Daddy,
of which you speak a lot?'
'It's proper music, son,
and they, for years, took centre spot.
Their full name was The Beatles:
Paul, Ringo, George and John;
Paul and Ringo still around,
the others sadly gone.'

'What is this 'taping' Daddy;
a useful thing, no doubt?'
'Ah, son, it means the telly;
recording when you're out.
We used a clever spool
to store a show when it was on.
But digital is now the way
and all of these have gone.'

'And what about that song you like,
by pop group 10CC?
'Someone waiting by the phone?'
That makes no sense to me.'
'Ah son, there wasn't always
a phone to carry round.

In olden days the telephone
was anchored to the ground.'

'But Daddy it sounds awful!
How ever did you cope?
You must now be so happy
and in the future hope?'
'In some ways, son, it's better,
with this technology.
But when we weren't all glued to screens
our lives seemed somehow free.

We'd climb trees in the forest,
play conkers in the fall,
in playgrounds knees and heads were grazed
but no one thought at all
to drag us to the doctor.
We wanted just to play
for many hours; meals were missed
and we had fun all day.'

91. THANK YOU

Have you tried to learn to speak
other languages, like Greek?
'Efcharistó' if you please,
to them means 'thank you.' But 'merci''s

the word for this in French and Persian.
In these countries words are merging.
To a Pole 'dziękuję' say
in appreciative way.

'Arigatou' in Japan,
is said, when grateful, if you can.
Danke schön for German friends.
'Kiitos' will avoid offence

in Finland, somewhere longer words
are normal. And ensure they've heard:
'diolch yn fawr iawn' in Wales.
Next, 'spasiba' seldom fails

to let a Russian know you're glad.
All these words could drive you mad.
When you're stuck and hit a wall;
can't communicate at all,

and you've travelled many miles,
know that all you need's a smile.
There's no place where this offends;
so now you have some brand new friends.

92. SCHOOL

Happy memories I have of school,
though never learned to master a slide rule.
I'm still not sure 'bout trigonometry.
And matrices remain a mystery.

Latin might not anymore be uttered,
but handy when in legal matters muttered.
Everyone learns French but still can't chatter.
We think when we're abroad it doesn't matter.

Some tiresome books we plough through for exams,
and then forget it all, 'cos now we can.
Apologies to Shakespeare and his sort.
I tried to like his plays, for sure one ought.

But this is stuff I really can't abide,
preferring PE class and things outside;
avoiding cigs and drugs and all things bad,
and bike shed interactions with the lads.

I'd like to thank the teachers for the ed-
-ucation for my job that keeps me fed,
and now allows me time to write in rhymes,
I hope at school you too had happy times.

93. MEDIA STORIES

'Wife lifts car in multi-storey',
'gran finds hods of cash',
'dad and son fall off a bus',
and 'mother grows some hash'.

You have to be a relative
to get into the news.
If you're a woman or a man
it's not enough to use

your story to sell media.
Even if a child's
a planet-saving genius,
this tale won't be compiled.

Categorisation
has become obligatory
of family relationships
to sell a worthy story.

Imagine if this were not so
and headlines could appear
of people most astonishing,
their family not here.

'Bloke rides bike to Timbuktu'.
'Lass grows giant pimple'.
'Chap solves question 42'.
Would it were that simple.

Soon we'll have 'great aunt does time',
'half-sis deals some dope',
'ma-in-law does ironman'
and 'Step-bro is new Pope'.

94. GEORDIE LASSES

It's Thursday night, they've all been paid,
it's time to venture forth.
For sure you'll be amazed to see
what girls wear in the north.

And not just in the summer,
they're in town without a wrap;
they party hard the whole night
in their gownless evening strap.

They hunt in packs, all tottering;
which bar will they next choose,
pouting at the bouncers,
insulated by the booze.

And when at last the time has come
to wend their merry way,
it's late at night, no coats in sight
and now they're going to pay.

They shiver in their flimsy garb,
much goosebumped flesh exposed.
In taxi ranks they huddle wishing
they'd put on more clothes.

We know that peer pressure means that
none will dare to speak
of dressing for the weather,
so it's same again next week.

95. BRITISH UNDERSTATEMENT

'Tis but a flesh wound,' Pythons jest.
At understatement we're the best.
When discussing the weather or injury,
we Brits dislike hyperbole.
If you're feeling bright and gay,
you'll say, when asked how're you today,

'I'm OK', 'fine', 'middling to fair',
'I'm good,' a millennial will declare.
But gradually the USA
ensures its lingo comes our way.
whooping, hollering, much loud cheer
now feature often over here.

No show's complete unless we see,
extreme sentimentality.
To older folk it isn't done
to show your joy when having fun.
Instead keep your expression dour;
one eyebrow raise like Roger Moore.

96. LIVING IN GOOD TIMES

Cures for cancer, mobile phones.
Inside toilets, agile drones.
Supermarkets selling booze,
Foreign travel; fancy cruise.
We never knew, more's the pity,
such diverse ethnicity.
Avocados, chicken wraps.
Not sliced white and boring baps.

Music with us on the go.
Silence, hard to come by now.
Parking in the town was free;
not so many cars, you see.
Wanting good remuneration,
you'd work hard at education.
None got rich with little slog,
posting pics or lifestyle blog.

IT games not yet a thing;
kids still played outside on swings.
Massive BMIs were rare;
now you see them everywhere.
Sunday trading, all shops closed.
Now restrictions not imposed.
You have all the shopping power;
purchase stuff at any hour.

Rudimentary ethnic food
back then wasn't very good.
Curry meant a dash of powder.
Our exotic cheese was gouda.
Eating clean – some think they oughta –
used to mean 'been rinsed with water.'
Nostalgic recollection ended,
life now has much to commend it.

97. NEWSPAPERS

What you've been reading is not always true;
your newspaper might have error or two.
It's just a wee slip, as they're not partisan
in stories 'bout spouses and cousins and gran.
When pets, like wee Tiddles, were rescued last night,
reporting and printing is usually right.

Perhaps their approach is a little more skewed
when writing 'bout politics, climate and food.
Agendas depend on to whom they're in hock.
The story is slanted when Ed's taking stock.
Political heavies, industrial clout;
a tactical whisper; some info's left out.

The words saying one thing, another will mean.
A story is dropped if events supervene.
And sensitive items slipped in carefully
on days of big news like a Queen's Jubilee.
It's cleverly done, as if it's been coded.
We still have free speech, but it's being eroded.

98. PRIME MINISTER MAY

There was a Prime Minister May
who tried to give people their way.
When it came to Brexit
some folk tried to hex it.
And what happened next, I can't say.

A London Mayor called Boris Johnson
Ex-MP for Henley was once on
the telly to say
he'll be PM one day.
To those in his way: move along son.

At number eleven there's fun;
Mr Hammond is doing his sums.
Concerned for the coffers,
he's open to offers.
But this side of Brexit there're none.

And what about Jeremy Corbyn
and matters of state he's absorbing.
Not just manhole covers;
he's thinking of others.
There's quite like him no one before been.

99. QUIZZES

Capitals, kings and plays by the Bard;
knowledge of these shows that you have worked hard.
You'll function at quizzes while most scratch their head,
when asked about stuff that as kids they have read.

By such folk on telly I'm greatly impressed;
some get answers right even when they have guessed.
Remember when Bamber respectfully probed?
But Jeremy's style is to fluster the bold.

He's not quite so harsh when some science occurs;
he skirts past this gingerly and then demurs.
Not sure why it's praised to know 'bout made-up stuff;
like Greek myths and legends, you surely could bluff.

But when about quantum mechanics and quarks,
and gluons and mesons, you make some remarks
like 'bottom' and 'strange', the words you have chosen
are bound to confuse, like the tale of Higgs boson.

100. CHILDREN'S TELLY CHARACTERS

Winnie the Pooh is loved by us all;
it's ageless and makes people smile.
If you can remember the Flowerpot Men,
you must have been here for a while.

Some are too young to remember the house
of Hector the affable dog.
They'll then be surprised that he chose to commune
with Zsazsa the cat, and a frog.

All folk are acquainted with Paddington Bear;
from darkest Peru he arrived.
And further away, far flung from our Earth,
there's news that the Clangers survive.

In diverse locations good stories are heard
'bout colourful folk on TV.
There's even a chap called SpongeBob SquarePants
who lives with his snail in the sea.

We have to admire what has been achieved
with plasticine shaped to express
a repertoire worthy of actors of note
by Wallace and Gromit, no less.

Homer and Bart and Lisa and Marge
teach lots about stuff in the States.
There's always a moral in tales that we're told
of these folk and their yellow mates.

I haven't forgotten the Wombles or Tom,
or Jerry or Bagpuss or Pat
the Postman or Scooby or Shaggy or Bugs,
or Pluto or Goofy. And that

is all I have time for, apart from a nod
to Dougal and Florence; it's said
the folk in the roundabout often were told
by Zebedee, 'It's time for bed.'

ABOUT THE AUTHOR

The author is a retired GP who lives in the northeast of England with one husband and one cat. This is her first foray into writing. The poems began while spending time with her father during his last illness. He was a great source of inspiration and encouragement. She hopes to entertain and gently provoke by writing about all manner of topics in a light-hearted way.

Printed in Great Britain
by Amazon